MAKE YOUR YEAR A LIVING SUCCESS GOALS WORKBOOK

Your Goal Setting Guide to a More Successful Life

PAMELA CARMICHAEL

Copyright © 2017 by Pamela Carmichael
All rights reserved.

No part of this publication may be reproduced, distributed or transmitted in any form or by any means, including photocopying, recording or other electronic or mechanical methods, without the prior written permission of the publisher, except in the case of brief quotations embodied in critical reviews, and certain other non-commercial uses permitted by copyright law.

For permission requests, write to the publisher, addressed to "Attention: Permissions Coordinator" at pamc@pamelavcarmichael.com

Disclaimer: This is an informational guide and is not intended as a substitute for legal, financial or other professional services. Take responsibility as a reader to consult a variety of sources and learn more about personal development strategies. While every effort has been made to make this guide accurate, it may contain typographical and content errors. The information expressed herein is the opinion of the author, and is not intended to reflect upon any particular person or company. The author and publisher shall have no responsibility or liability with respect to any loss or damage caused, or alleged to be caused, by the information or application of the information contained in this guide. It is hope that this content will serve you well as you take action towards achieving your goals and living out a Godly life.

For permission requests, write to the publisher at pamc@pamelavcarmichael.com

Ordering information:
Quantity sales. Special discounts are available on quantity purchases by corporations, associations and others. For details, contact the "Special Sales Department" at pamc@pamelavcarmichael.com

Published by LIVING SUCCESS PUBLISHERS

ISBN-13: 978-0-9917850-3-2
ISBN-10: 0991785037

Printed in United States of America

Unless otherwise indicated, all Scripture quotations are taken from the New King James Version. Copyright © 1982 by Thomas Nelson, Inc. Used by permission. All rights reserved.

Scripture quotations marked AB are taken from The Amplified Bible. Copyright © 1965, 1987, by the Zondervan Corporation. Used by permission. All rights reserved.

Scripture quotations marked MSG are taken from THE MESSAGE. Copyright © by Eugene H. Peterson 1993, 1994. 1995, 1996, 2000, 2001, 2002. Used by permission of NavPress Publishing Group.

Scripture quotations marked NASB are taken from the New American Standard Bible, © Copyright 1960, 1962, 1963, 1968, 1971, 1972, 1973, 1975, 1977, 1995 by the Lockman Foundation. Used by permission.

Scripture quotations marked NIV are taken from the HOLY BIBLE, NEW INTERNATIONAL VERSION®. Copyright © 1973, 1978, 1984, Biblica. Used by permission of Zondervan. All rights reserved.

Table of Contents

WELCOME! 5

YOUR FREE BONUS: ADDITIONAL 90-DAY PLANNING SHEETS FOR YOUR LIVING SUCCESS YEAR! 6

HOW TO USE THIS WORKBOOK 7

WHAT MADE THE YEAR GREAT (OR NOT SO GREAT)? 8

DEAR GOD 12

WHAT IS GOD'S WORD TO YOU IN THIS COMING YEAR? 14

WHERE AM I TODAY? 15

WHAT AREAS OF MY LIFE SHOULD I FOCUS ON? 15

CREATE YOUR VISION BOARD 16

MY DREAM LIST FOR THIS YEAR 19

DEFINE YOUR GOALS 21

WHAT'S YOUR WHY? 22

CALENDAR YOUR GOALS 23

WHAT'S YOUR NEXT STEPS – BEGIN THE "HOW TO" 25

MAKING THE VISION PLAIN – MY GOALS IN 3D 26

PRAY THE WORD 39

TAKE A PERSONAL RETREAT 41

GET ACCOUNTABLE 42

WEEKLY, MONTHLY & QUARTERLY PLANNING 44

JOURNAL YOUR THOUGHTS 45

90-DAY REVIEW & PLAN: _____ 46

30-DAY CHALLENGE – MONTH: _____ 49

MONTH: _____ 50

30-DAY CHALLENGE – MONTH: _____ 60

MONTH: _____ 61

30-DAY CHALLENGE – MONTH: _____ 71

MONTH: _____ 72

THIS YEAR & BEYOND – YOUR LIFE STORY 82

CONGRATULATIONS & THANK YOU! 85

PLEASE SHARE YOUR EXPERIENCE 86

OTHER RESOURCES 89

ABOUT PAMELA 90

Welcome!

Congrats on taking this time to design your year ahead with the Lord. Yes, with the Lord. You can take this step on your own, as many do and achieve some measure of success, but I encourage you to take this journey with the Lord's guidance. Of course, He knows best for you. He has blessed you with abilities, gifts, education, resources, and people that are unique to you and He wants you to make the best of them all.

As you go through this workbook it is my sincerest desire and prayer that you will not only complete the steps but you will take action on what you have crafted and experience living success through Christ your Strength, Ever-Present Help and Friend.

Get started creating your Living Success Year!

Live Success!

Pamela Carmichael

Your Free Bonus: Additional 90-day Planning Sheets for Your Living Success Year!

Before you begin reading this book, I have a free bonus to offer you.

To keep the momentum going once I have completed the first 90 days, I print the 90-day planning sheets so I can remain focused on my goals and plan. I try not to leave anything to chance or that would cause me to have any kind of excuse for not forging ahead with my goals.

Since I want you to keep moving forward, I am going to share my planning sheets with you. All you have to do is sign up for my email list and I will send you the link to access it. Easy.

To receive your free access link please sign up below, it only takes a second.

Go to this link to get the planning sheets – https://www.pamelavcarmichael.com/resources/living-success-goals-workbook-90-day-planning-sheets/

Once you sign up, you will emailed access to the planning sheets. Before the end of 90 days, make sure to print these off and place in a folder to use as soon as you've completed this workbook. It will help you keep on target with your goals and track your progress.

I am elated to help you on this success journey.

To Your Living Success!

PamelaC

How to Use This Workbook

- ✓ Fill in the sections as best as you possibly can.

- ✓ Write from the heart.

- ✓ Keep this workbook close at hand to review on a regular basis – daily, weekly, monthly and quarterly.

- ✓ Get visual – you can take some parts and post them where you can see them daily. For example, your dream board and your dream list for this year are great sign posts.

- ✓ Use the weekly, monthly and quarterly sections to plan and to keep on track of your progress. Be sure to make an appointment with yourself to do these.

- ✓ Take bite-size chunks toward your goals. You can't do it all at once so break the goals into smaller, manageable tasks.

- ✓ Take action. The whole purpose of goal setting is to outline a plan that you can act on. So do just that!

- ✓ Enjoy the journey. Along the way there may be some ups and downs but approach each step with an open heart and a willingness to learn.

- ✓ Be accountable. Share you goals with one or two close friends or peers who have similar interests and who you can mastermind with to gain insight.

- ✓ In all you do: ask, obey and trust the Lord. He knows what is best for you!

"Trust in the Lord with all your heart; do not depend on your own understanding. Seek his will in all you do, and he will show you which path to take." Proverbs 3:5-6 (NLT)

WHAT MADE THE YEAR GREAT (OR NOT SO GREAT)?

This is the time to celebrate the past, give thanks to God, say goodbye to the ugliness of the past and pave the way for a good future. Please don't dwell on failures, or shoulda-coulda's but learn from the past and do things differently this time around.

Ask yourself the following questions to help you review the previous year.

What am I most happy about in last year?

What kind of sweet surprises did I experience?

Three things that I am most grateful to God for doing in my life.

What new dream or goal did I achieve?

Looking back, what would I have done differently?

Where did I let fear hold me back from accomplishing a goal I had?

Are there any regrets or disappointments that I keep rehashing and need to let go of?

Is there any unfinished business that I need to resolve? When will I do it? (E.g. relationship resolution or forgiveness, apologies, goals not yet achieve, de-cluttering, financial reviews, etc.)

What new and inspiring people did I meet?

Who would I like to get closer to in the coming year? (Remember, you are the average of the five people you spend most time with. Choose wisely!)

_____
_____
_____
_____
_____
_____
_____

One thing that helps me release the past is to write a letter to the Lord. Every December 31st morning, I would rise up earlier to spend time with the Lord and with this specific task in mind. Usually I would focus on what I am thankful for. But often I would recall some of the events of the year and write how I saw the Lord working in these times for my benefit. Through this writing there would be pauses to even verbally give thanks, to wipe the tears from my eyes and to just bask in the presence of God.

On the next page, take a few moments to write a love letter to God for all He is done in your life in the previous year. You can either start off with "Dear God" or you can scratch that greeting and start with your own.

Dear God ...

WHAT IS GOD'S WORD TO YOU IN THIS COMING YEAR?

This is the time to pray and seek God for a word that will sustain you throughout the New Year. In some churches, the pastor may declare the Word of the Lord for the coming year. If you believe that Word is for you, then use it. However, if your church doesn't do this or if you believe that there is a specific word more pertinent to your life; then seek God for it.

Trust me, you will find that the Word you receive is just what you need when challenges arise, when you feel low in spirit or as a reminder of God's promise and faithfulness to you.

Write the Word of God to you for this year in the space below along with a scriptural reference. Here's an example...

The Year of God's Favor

Psalm 5:12 "For You, O Lord, will bless the righteous; with favor You will surround him as with a shield."

The Year Of

_____

_____

"Your word is a lamp to my feet and a light to my path." Psalm 119:105 (NKJV)

WHERE AM I TODAY?

Rate yourself in each of the following life areas. **Where do you find yourself today?** On a scale of 1 to 10 with 10 being the most satisfied and 1 being the least satisfied, write the number inside each area. After you've done this, rate yourself in each of these areas in the future. **Where would you like to be at the end of this year?** What's your dream improvement mark? Write that rating outside each area.

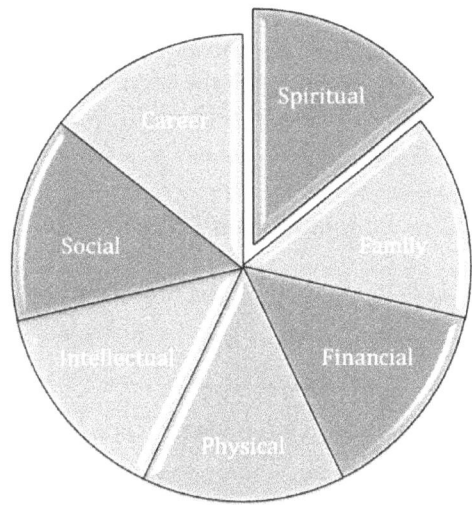

Although there are several areas, there are some you may want to work on or place more emphasis on improving. List the areas of your life that you want to focus your attention on this year. You don't need to list all, focus on what needs priority and that the Lord is leading you to take action on.

WHAT AREAS OF MY LIFE SHOULD I FOCUS ON?

1.
2.
3.
4.
5.
6.
7.

CREATE YOUR VISION BOARD

Have fun with this! The purpose of this step is to create a visual of your dreams. **The more you see the more you act on what you see.** Sometimes when life gets a little challenging and the dream starts to fade within your dream board will help to encourage you and revive your dreams.

God gives us visuals also to remind us of His promises and faithfulness to us:

- ✓ The rainbow in the sky symbolizing God's promise never to flood the earth again
- ✓ The sand on the seashore and the stars in the sky that reminded Abraham how great his descendants would be
- ✓ The star in the sky at the birth of our Lord Jesus Christ
- ✓ Of course, the written word of God filled with His promises and love letter to us

This step is another way of "writing the vision" so it is clear to you.

You will need a few things to do this board:

- ✓ A Bristol board or a scrapbook or for humble begins the page titled "My Vision Board"
- ✓ An extra page in the workbook (to make a mini board)
- ✓ Magazine, postcards, old books
- ✓ Images you can download from the internet (optional)
- ✓ Scissors and glue
- ✓ Marker (to write the title of your dream board or make other special markings)

Look for images that you can cut out or print. Make a collage with the pictures on the Bristol board or paper. Every day review your dream board and prayer about your goals (for direction and success).

Alternatively another option is to write out your vision letting your thoughts flow using the page titled, "My Vision in the Clouds". In each cloud, write down your immediate thoughts based on the words in the each cloud. Every success in life starts with an idea.

Enjoy the process and dream with God. Equally important is to use the option that best suits your personality and learning style.

My Vision Board

My Vision in the Clouds

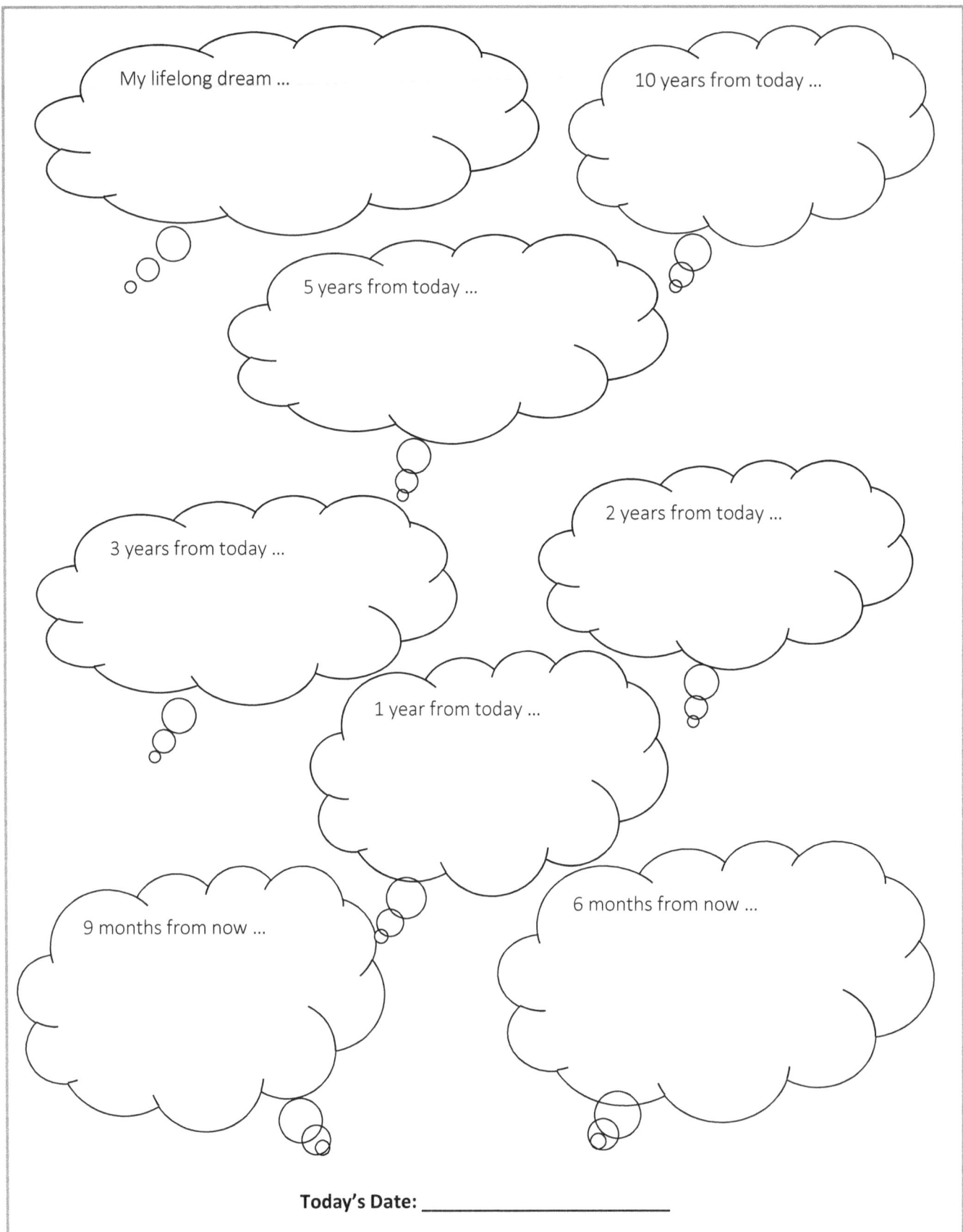

My Dream List for This Year

"The plans of the mind and orderly thinking belong to man, but from the Lord comes the [wise] answer of the tongue. All the ways of a man are pure in his own eyes, but the Lord weighs the spirits (the thoughts and intents of the heart). Roll your works upon the Lord [commit and trust them wholly to Him; He will cause your thoughts to become agreeable to His will, and] so shall your plans be established and succeed." Prov. 16:1-3(AMP)

My pastor encouraged the church members every year to make a list of 12 things that we wanted to accomplish or that we wanted the Lord to do in our lives during the coming year. Every Dec-31 was climaxed with a time of praise and worship and testimonies, thanksgiving for the blessings of the year (goals accomplished, healings, relationships restored, etc.). Just before the New Year was ushered in we would pray over the 12 things we had on our list asking God to help us accomplish those goals. For me this event started long before the December 31 night service, I often spent the prior two weeks praying and thinking about what I would like my year ahead to look like for me and my family. This initial list was just the beginning as I would often find myself revising or amending as the Lord guided me during the year. At times there were items on the list that I would repeat year after year because they were longer term goals. Other goals I would soon come to realize weren't mine at all (maybe you've experience that, your heart wasn't into it you just thought it would be a good thing to accomplish☺). Certainly though, there were goals that I accomplished. In this exercise, focus on this year. At the end of the planner there is room to create longer term goals – Your Life Story.

You don't have to start with 12 dreams but maybe 7 to 9 may prove to be more manageable as some goals may take a longer time frame to work on than others.

Have fun here and be quick to write what's on your heart, you will have time to refine and define these later.

My Dream List (What Do I Want The Lord To Do In My Life This Year?)

DEFINE YOUR GOALS

Your dream list for this year was a great start but you have to do more than dream – you have to create goals to make the dreams become reality. Sure you could stop at your dream list but you would be doing yourself a disservice. There is more…

"A goal is a dream with a deadline." Napoleon Hill

Look back at the list you just created and make them more concrete. Let your goals be Specific, Measurable, Achievable, Relevant, Time sensitive.

It is not enough to say "I want to be healthier this year" or "I want to make more money" or "I want to grow closer to God." Your goals need to be specific, clear and have deadlines. You can better measure your progress by creating S.M.A.R.T. goals.

As an example, if you had on your Dream List for this year that you want to make more money, you'll need to get more real and specific about. Let's say you make $35,000 per year and want to increase that; then maybe you can write "I want to increase my income by $15,000 by the end of this year."

Look at it more definitively in an S.M.A.R.T. goal format:

I want	To increase my income	By $15,000	By end of the year
Who	What	Measurement	When
Specific	Specific	Measurable	Time sensitive
Personal assessment of the goal	Is it Achievable (or Attainable)?	Is it Relevant (to you)?	Is the "where" important to the goal? If Yes, note it.
This answer only you can give	Yes / No	Yes / No	Yes / No

Planning and goal setting is like a self-fulfilling prophecy and you want to write what you see inside of you. Be bold to write what you see inside and be as crystal clear as you can be. Start creating your goals on the sheets provided titled Goal No. 1 through to Goal No. 12.

Warning: This is a great start to goal setting BUT as a Christian, S.M.A.R.T. goals can be limiting. **Please don't limit what God has placed in your heart at the cost of being realistic by the world's standards. Your goals should stretch you and your faith in the Most High God you serve.** Check out the blog post I wrote entitled, *How to Make FAITH Goals Rather Than SMART Ones* **(http://www.pamelavcarmichael.com/how-to-make-faith-goals-rather-than-smart-ones/)**.

Tip: You may want to add a short version of your goal list to your smart phone so you have it with you at all times, to review, to pray about and to help you keep focused on the prize.

What's Your Why?

"... but one thing I do, forgetting those things which are behind and reaching forward to those things which are ahead, I press toward the goal for the prize of the upward call of God in Christ Jesus."
Philippians 3:13-14 (NKJV)

Sometimes you can get carried away with the excitement of a new season dawning. Like resolutions that you may start off buzzing to accomplish and then within a short period of time your enthusiasm and your resolution comes to a screeching halt. But I don't want that to happen to you this time. You have to keep the pace going – like Paul – you must keep pressing forward towards your prize. His goal was to win the prize (the blessing) that God gives to those who do His will. That should be your main aim too but at the same time you need to be specific as it pertains to your life. To do this you will need to have a compelling "Why" for each of your goals. Paul did – he was pressing *to reach the end of the race and receive the heavenly prize for which God, through Christ Jesus, is calling us.*

What about you, what are you pressing towards and why are you doing it? Why do you want to accomplish the goals you've created? Or asking this question another way... **What's the benefits of accomplishing these goals? What happens when I achieve this goal? How will I feel? What would it look like when this happens? Who benefits apart from me?**

For each goal, give a few compelling reason(s) why you want to complete them. If you cannot find at least two reasons for each goal, maybe you need to rethink if that goal is worth pursuing. There is a lot to think about but keep going.

CALENDAR YOUR GOALS

"Look carefully then how you walk! Live purposefully and worthily and accurately, not as the unwise and witless, but as wise (sensible, intelligent people), Making the very most of the time [buying up each opportunity], because the days are evil. Therefore do not be vague and thoughtless and foolish, but understanding and firmly grasping what the will of the Lord is." Ephesians 5:15-17 (AMP)

Here you begin to create a date visual of your goals for this year. Of course, each goal will take time to accomplish and if you think through each goal carefully you would have indicated some timelines at which you would like to accomplish them.

Get a large calendar; write down **when** you would like to complete each goal. One thing to remember is that you can't work all the time. Make sure that you take time off for personal retreats, family time or vacation, church events and remember to maximize on public holidays to get some rest. Ask the Lord to help you balance all the areas of your life and avoid stress and overworking.

Go ahead! A first step is to mark your calendar with all the important dates for the year e.g. birthdays, anniversaries, special occasions, public holidays, vacation time, etc. Whatever important dates are known to you now include them so that you can plan with them in mind. Second step is to add your **goal dates**. Get excited!

Tip: You can put these dates into any electronic calendar you have with timely reminders. So get out your smart phone or your online calendar and update it for this year.

Alternatively, if you need a big picture, get a wall calendar and post it where you can see it every day.

In addition to the calendar, you will find "**My Goals in Quarters**" page. The purpose of this page is to do big picture thinking of when you want to accomplish certain goals. You may find it useful if you like having an overview of your year in 90-day or quarterly groupings. This is optional and you can use it if you want to have a quick view of the year on one page; kind of like a one-page personal plan.

My Goals in Quarters

Q1	Q2

Q3	Q4

WHAT'S YOUR NEXT STEPS – BEGIN THE "HOW TO"

"Suppose you want to build a tower. You would first sit down and figure out what it costs. Then you would see if you have enough money to finish it. Otherwise, if you lay a foundation and can't finish the building, everyone who watches will make fun of you. They'll say, 'This person started to build but couldn't finish the job.'" — Luke 14:28-30 (GW)

Just like you would determine the cost of building a house, renovating or purchasing big ticket items, you need to know what is required – "the cost" – of accomplishing your goal. What is the process? What steps will you need to take? Who can you ask to help or who will you need to hire? What resources will you need? Where will you need to go in order to make this goal happen? The "Who", "What", "Where" and "When" is equal to the "How".

During this part of the goal setting process, don't get bogged down with too much detail just yet. Too much "to-do's" lead to overwhelm (trust me, I know). For each goal list at least three steps you can do to get you started. Make these date specific as well and don't just think, "I'll get to them soon enough." You will find that with the small steps accomplished each day and/or week you can ask yourself that question again and again, "What's my next steps?" You will create the momentum to move forward when you see the progress you're making.

Based on the goals you created, make a list of three things you can do right now to make your goal become a reality.

Tip: To accomplish anything big or small requires you to develop daily or weekly habits. You can write as many grandiose goals as you can but nothing comes to fruition without practicing daily habits. This takes the grace of God. Ask for God's help daily and be wise as you work towards it. Remember, go step by step with God at your side all the way.

MAKING THE VISION PLAIN – MY GOALS IN 3D

Then the Lord answered me, Write the vision. Make it clear on tablets so that anyone can read it quickly. The vision will still happen at the appointed time. It hurries toward its goal. It won't be a lie. If it's delayed, wait for it. It will certainly happen. It won't be late. — Habakkuk 2:2-3 (GW)

Now is your turn to make your vision become clearer to you. Now is time to get more specific about your dreams and turn them into goals. For each goal write the **What, Why, When and How**. Don't worry if you don't fill in all the blanks. For sure, you will revise this list during the year to tweak some of your plans and in some case to postpone or even cancel some of them. One thing to remember here is that this is a work-in-progress as your life progresses and changes. What may matter today may not a few months from now or a few years from now. That is not meant to dissuade you from planning but to remind you that your priorities can change. As the Lord leads you and you grow in Christ some of your plans will not matter as much as they did before.

I recommend that you really take time out (Selah) and ask the Holy Spirit to guide you as you prepare for this season and beyond.

Once you've done that. Take one page and create one goal strategy at a time.

Tip: Approach your goals little by little. To avoid overwhelm you may consider only working on your goals in 90-day chunks. So start off with your first quarter goals and then calendar some planning time each quarter to review and plan your next set of 90-day goals.

GOAL NO. 1

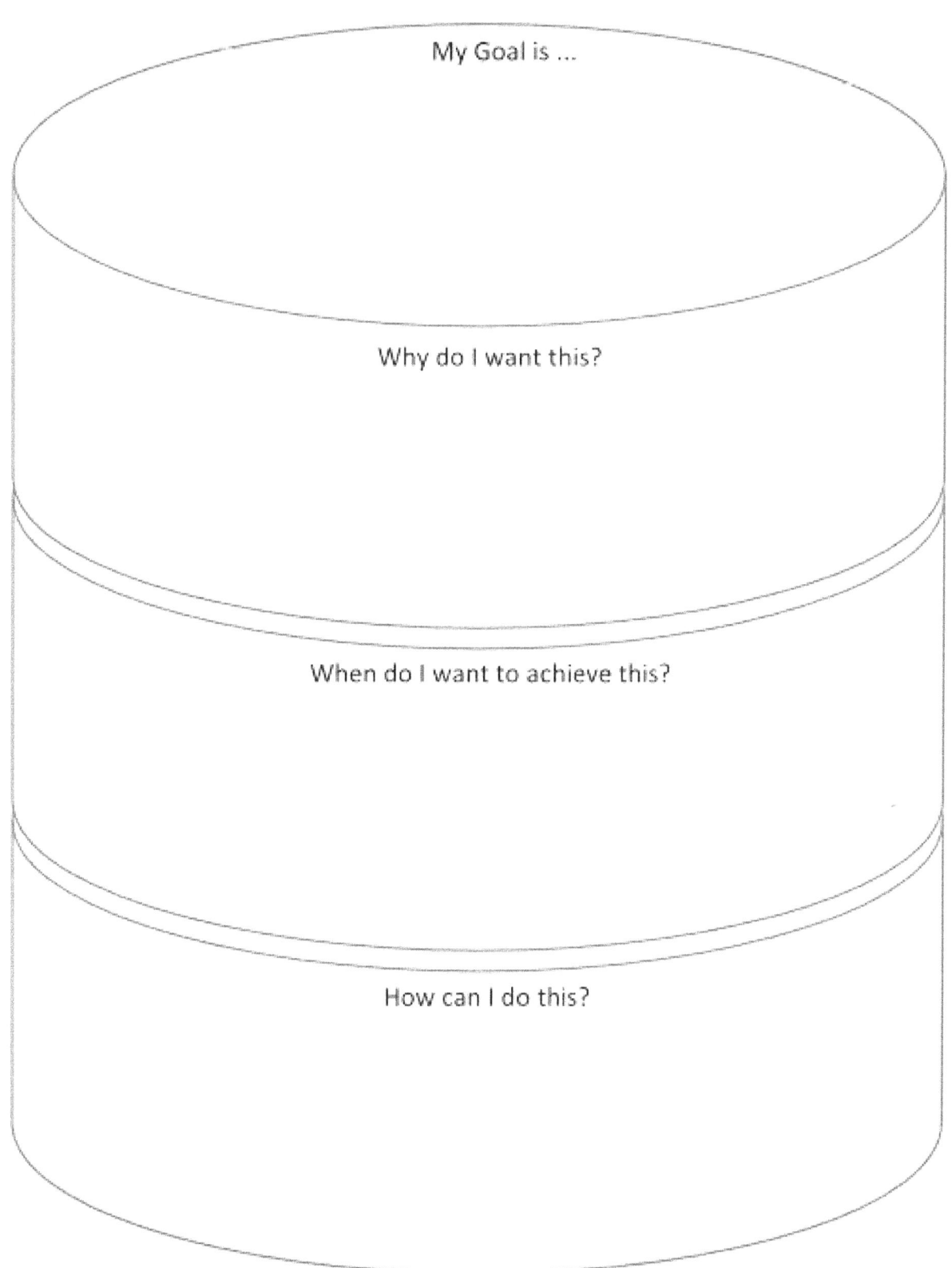

GOAL NO. 2

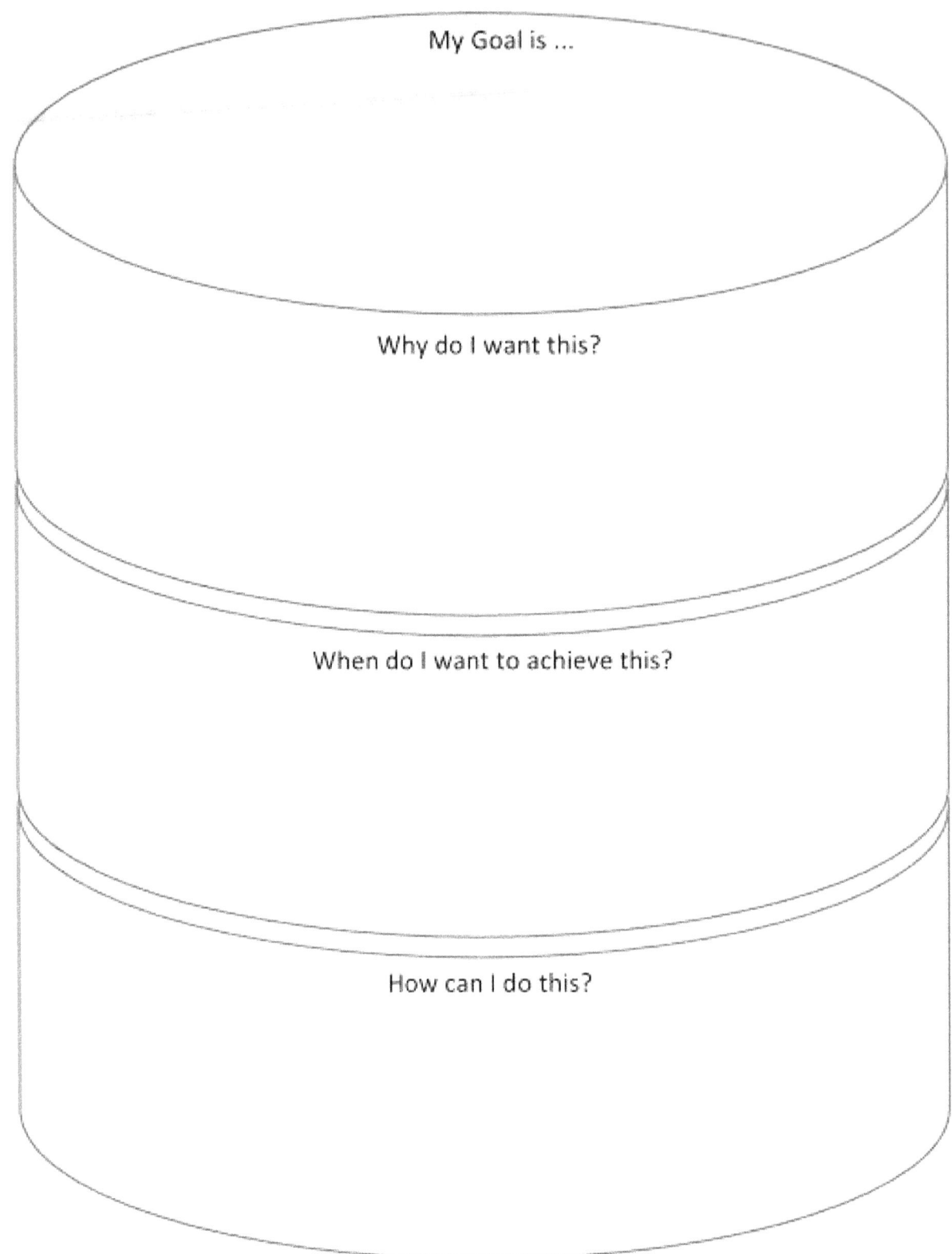

GOAL NO. 3

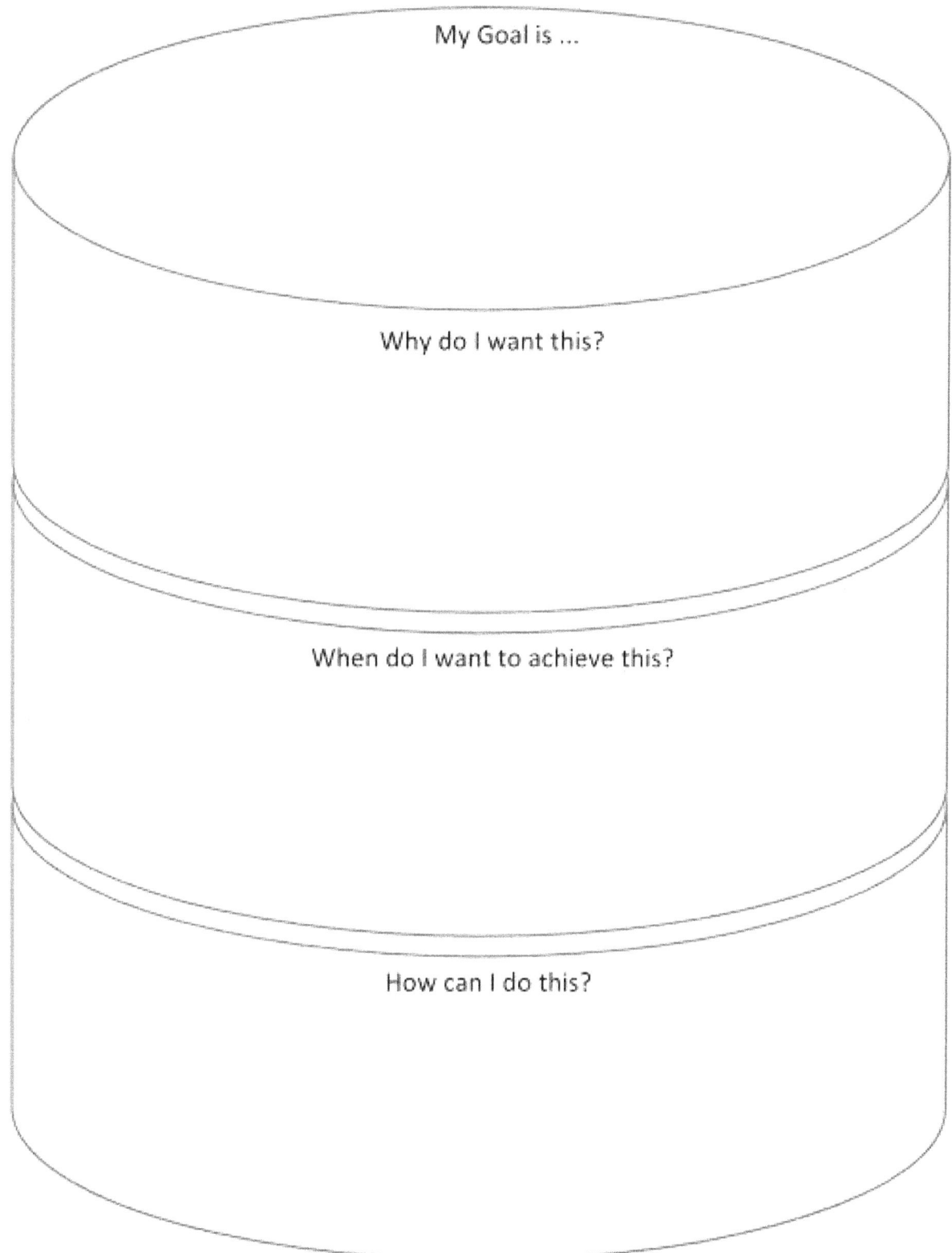

GOAL NO. 4

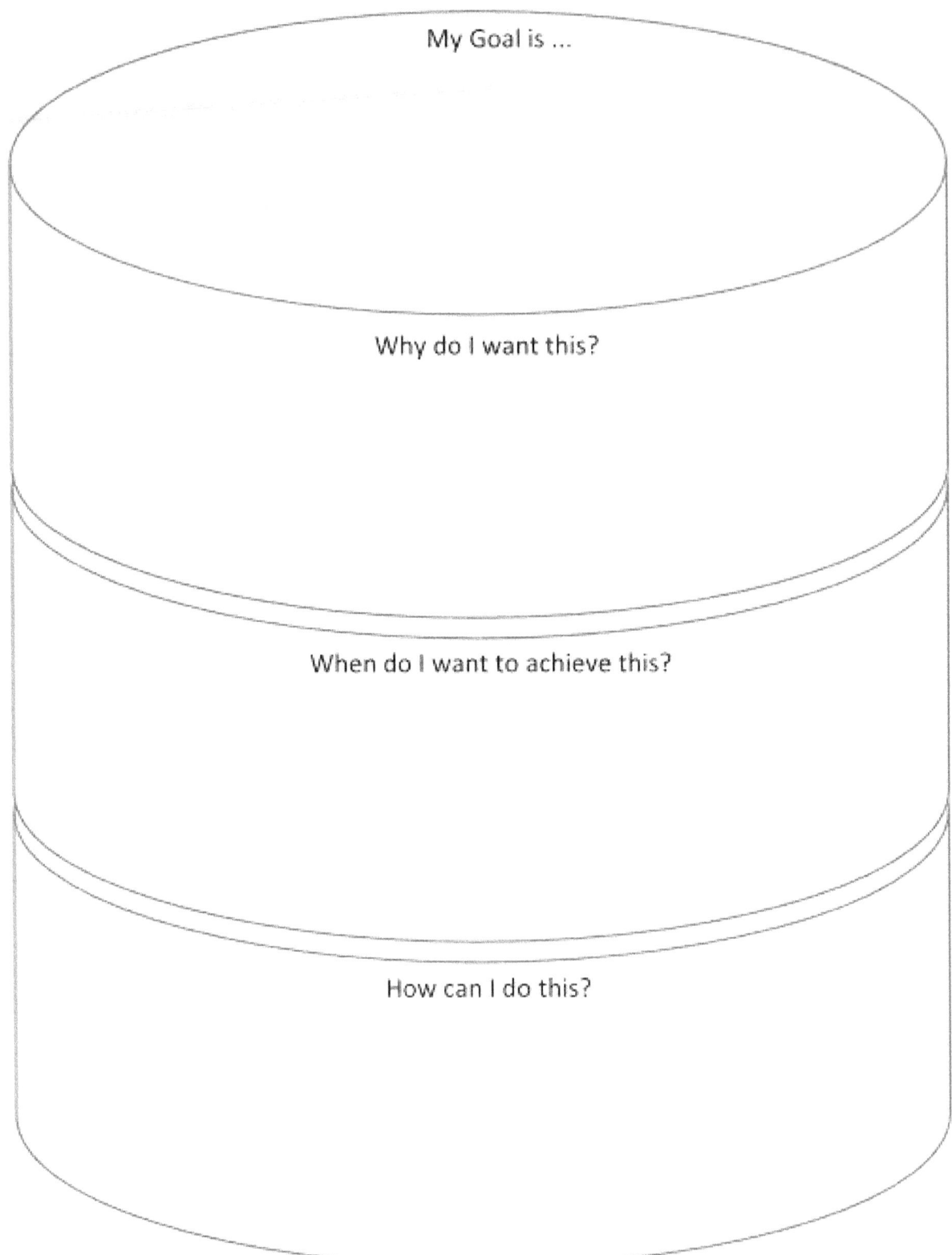

GOAL NO. 5

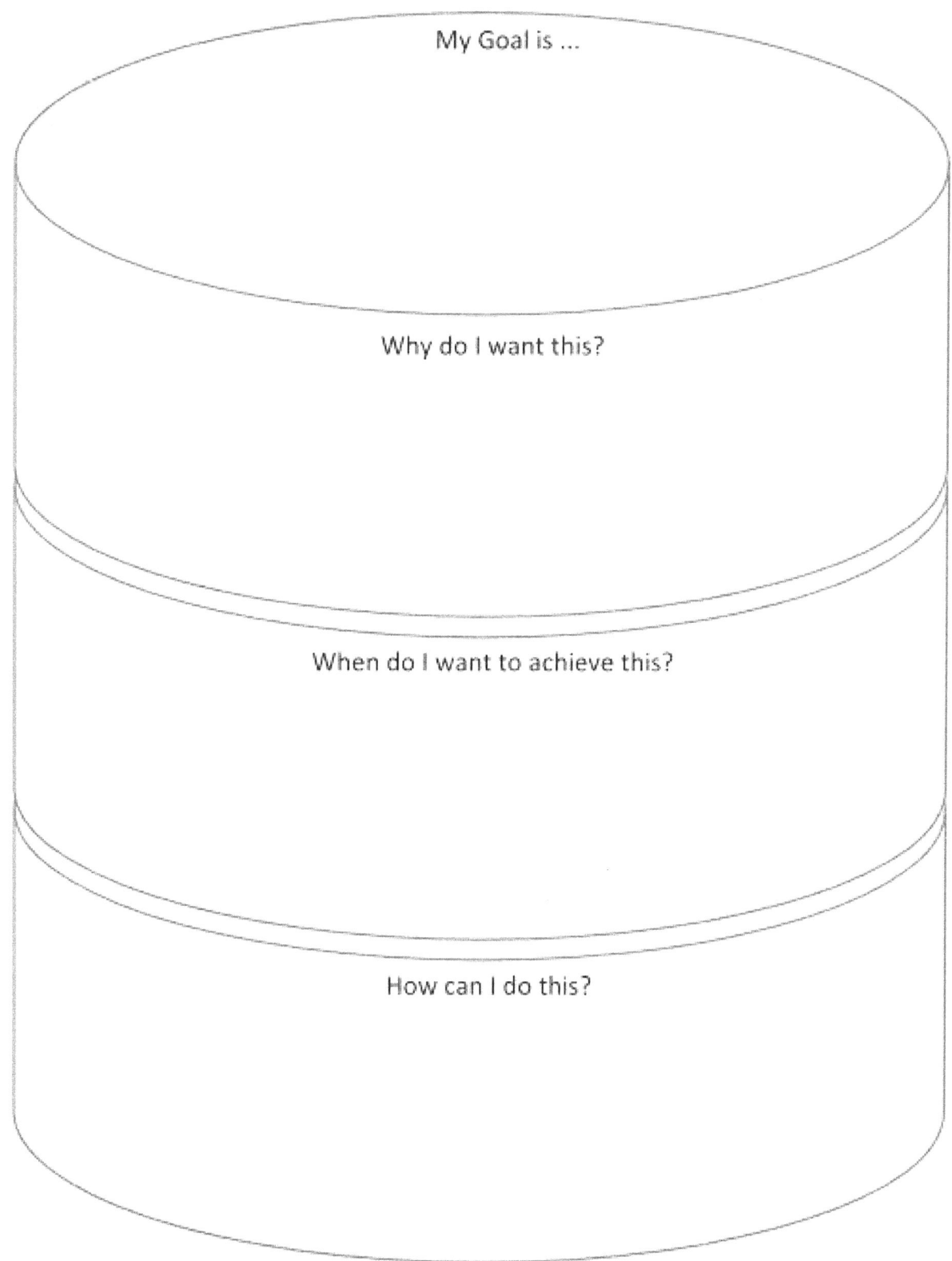

GOAL NO. 6

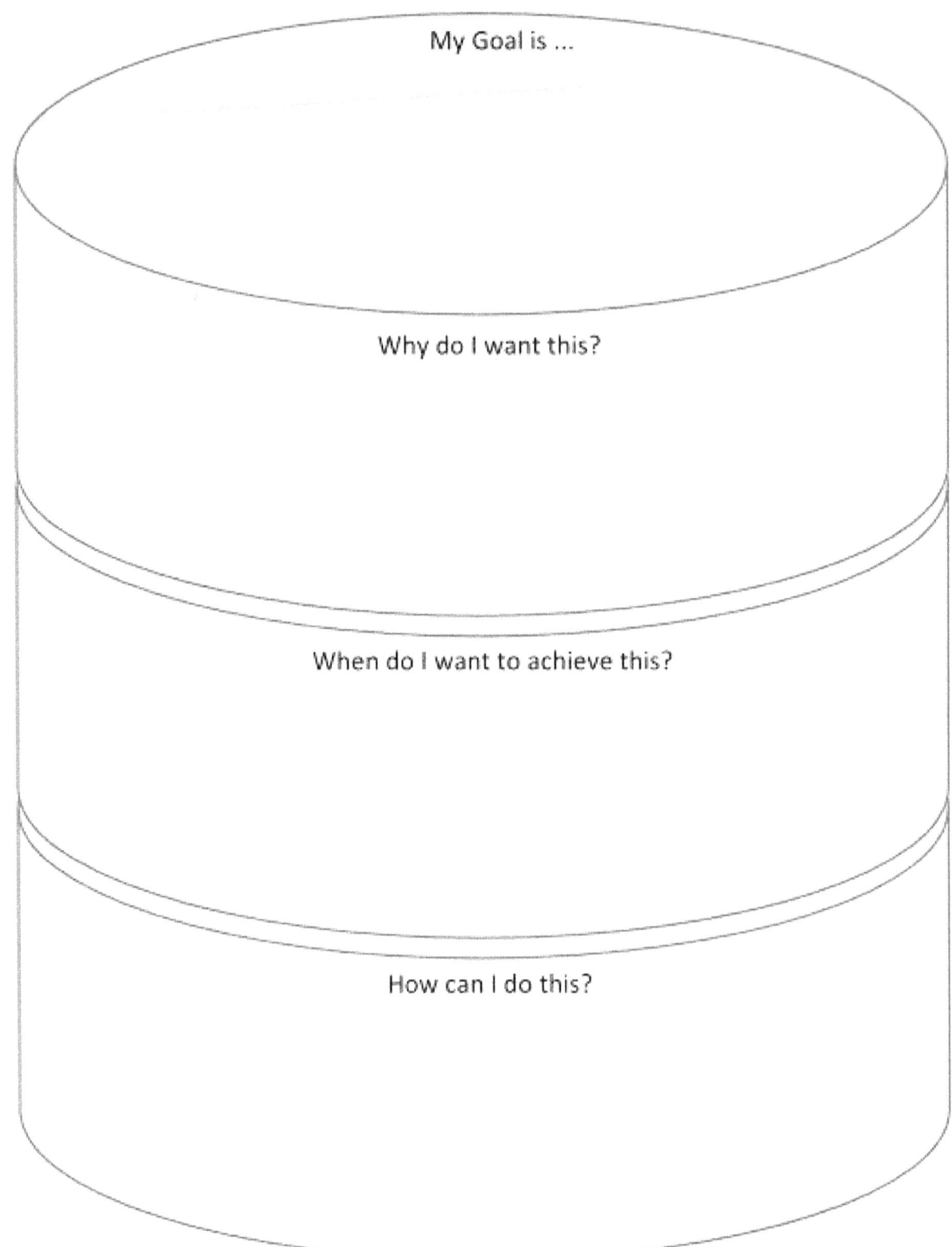

GOAL No. 7

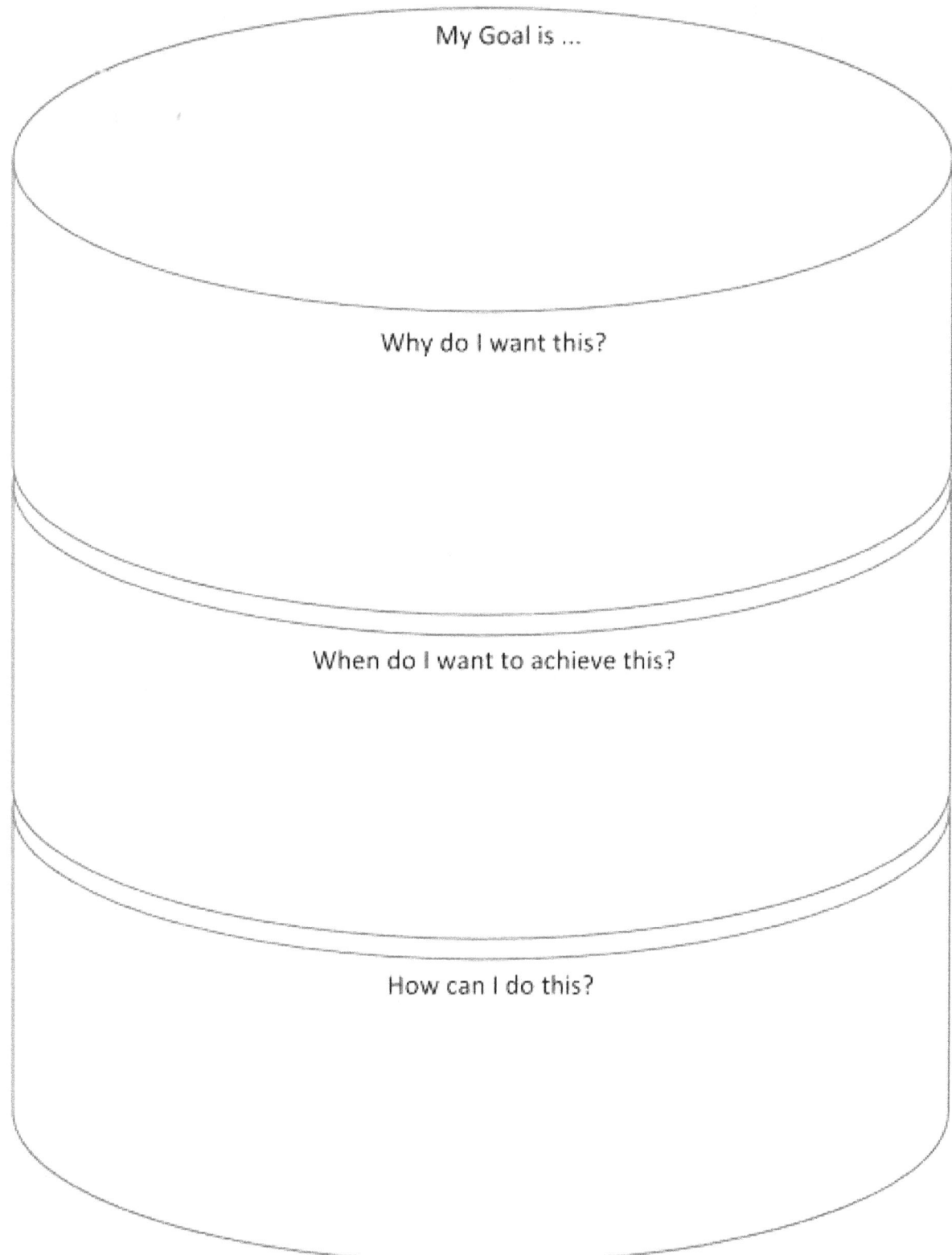

GOAL No. 8

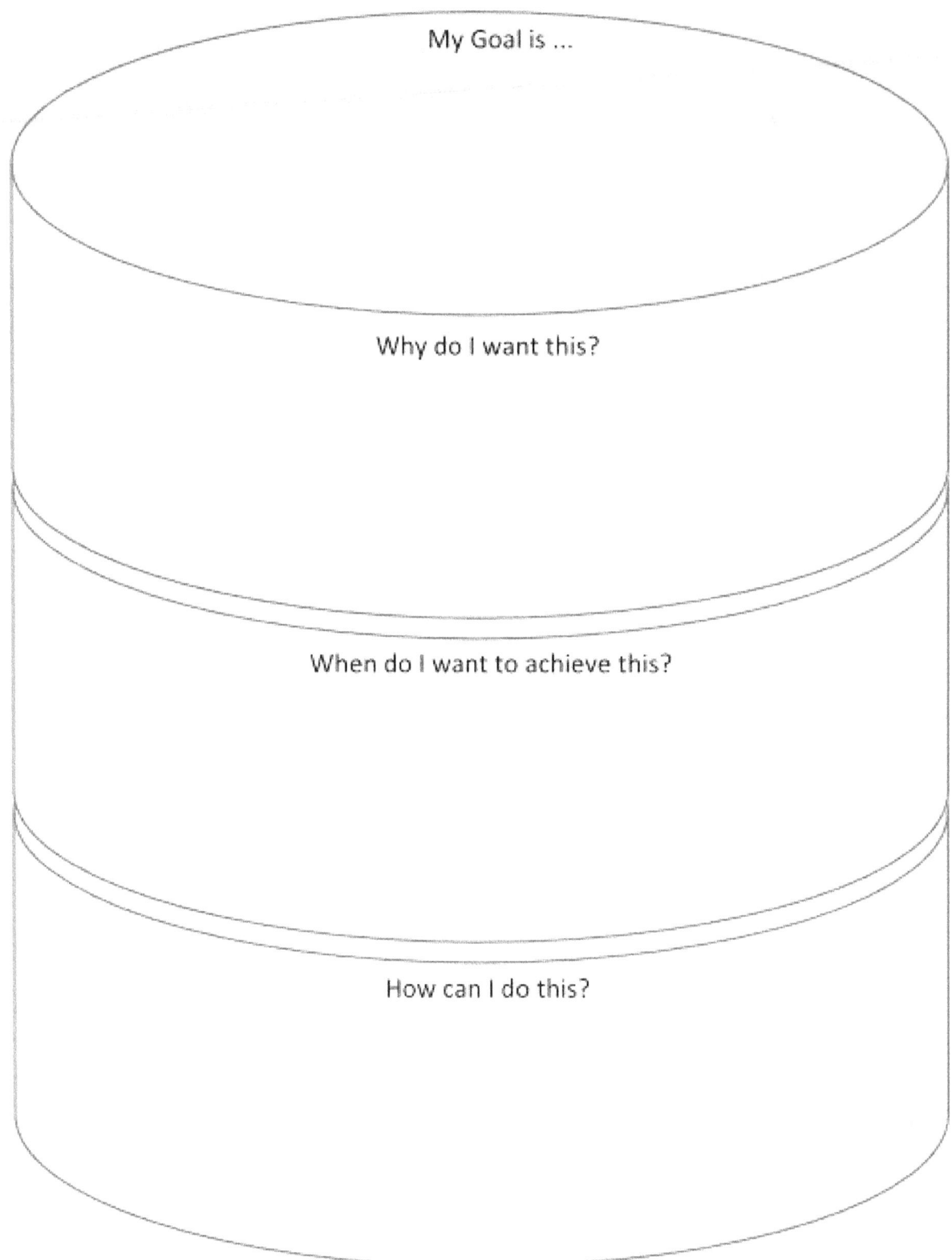

GOAL NO. 9

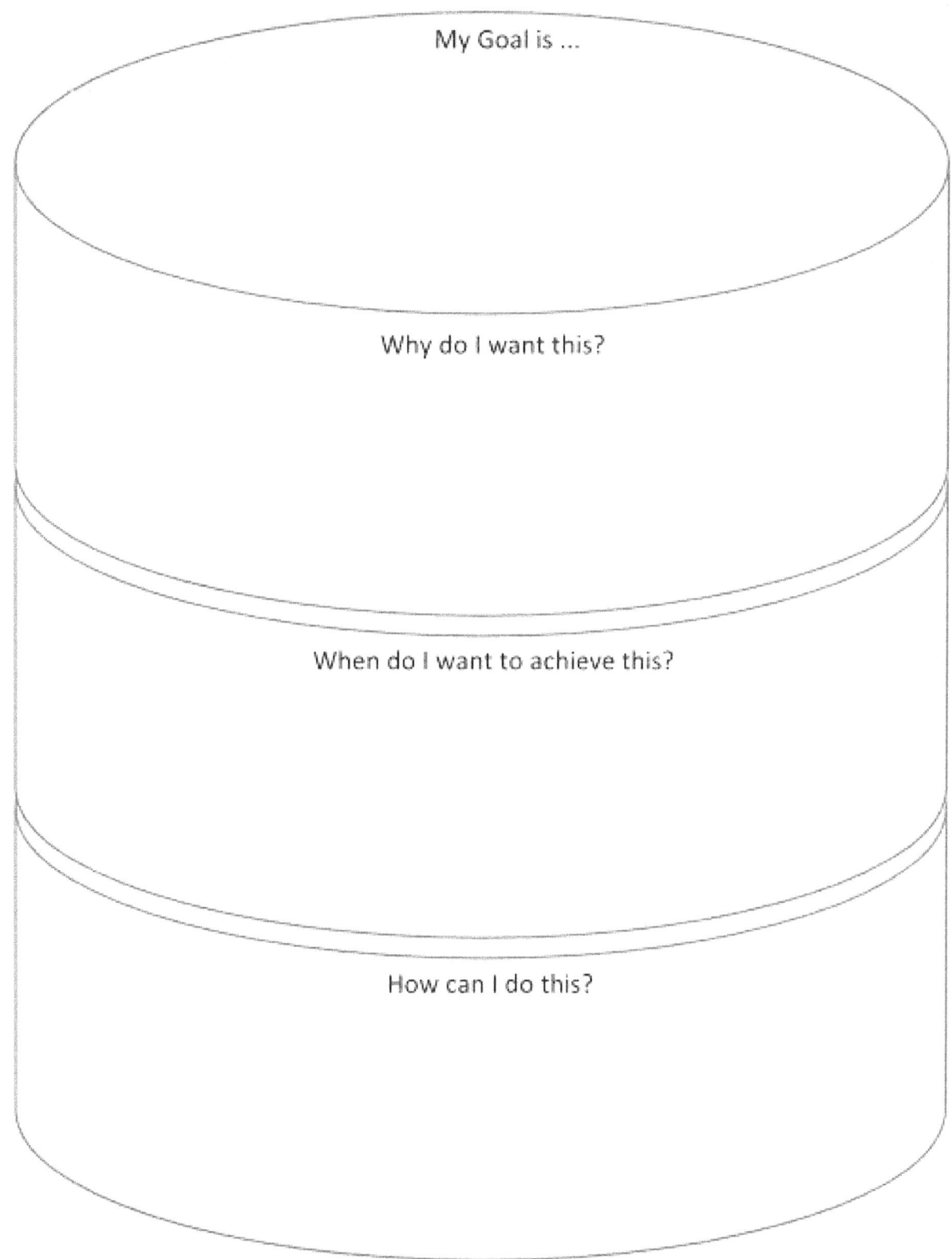

GOAL NO. 10

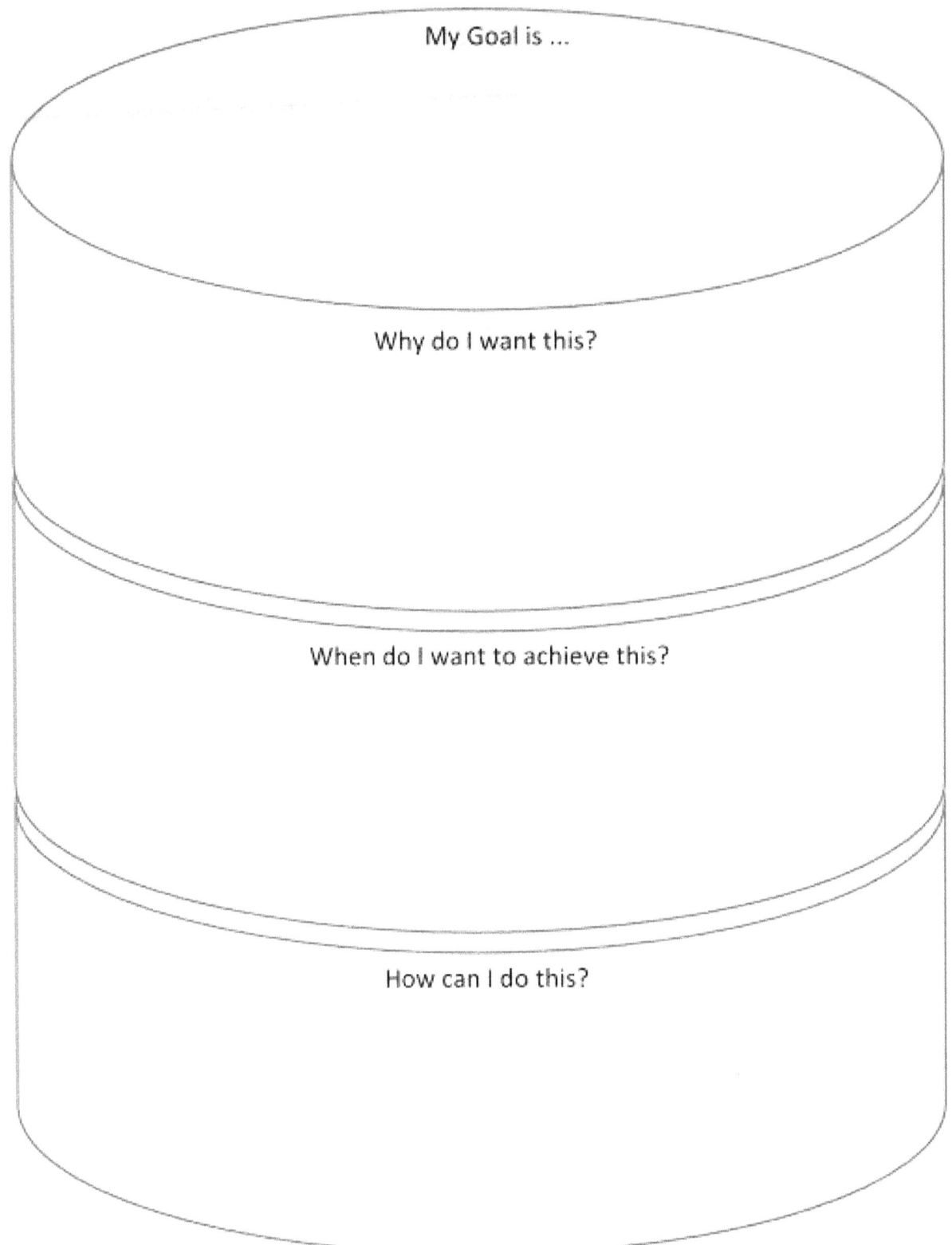

GOAL NO. 11

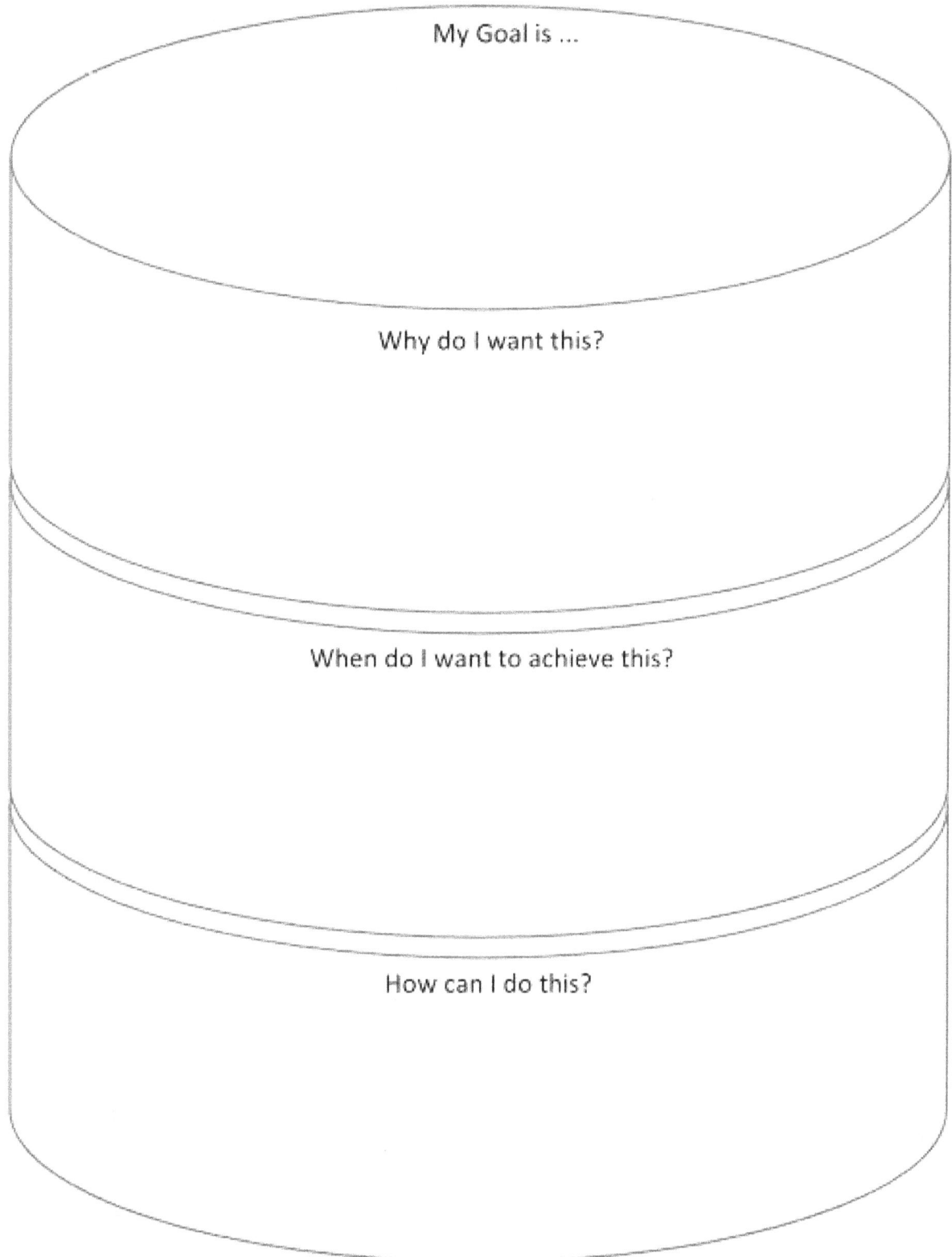

GOAL NO. 12

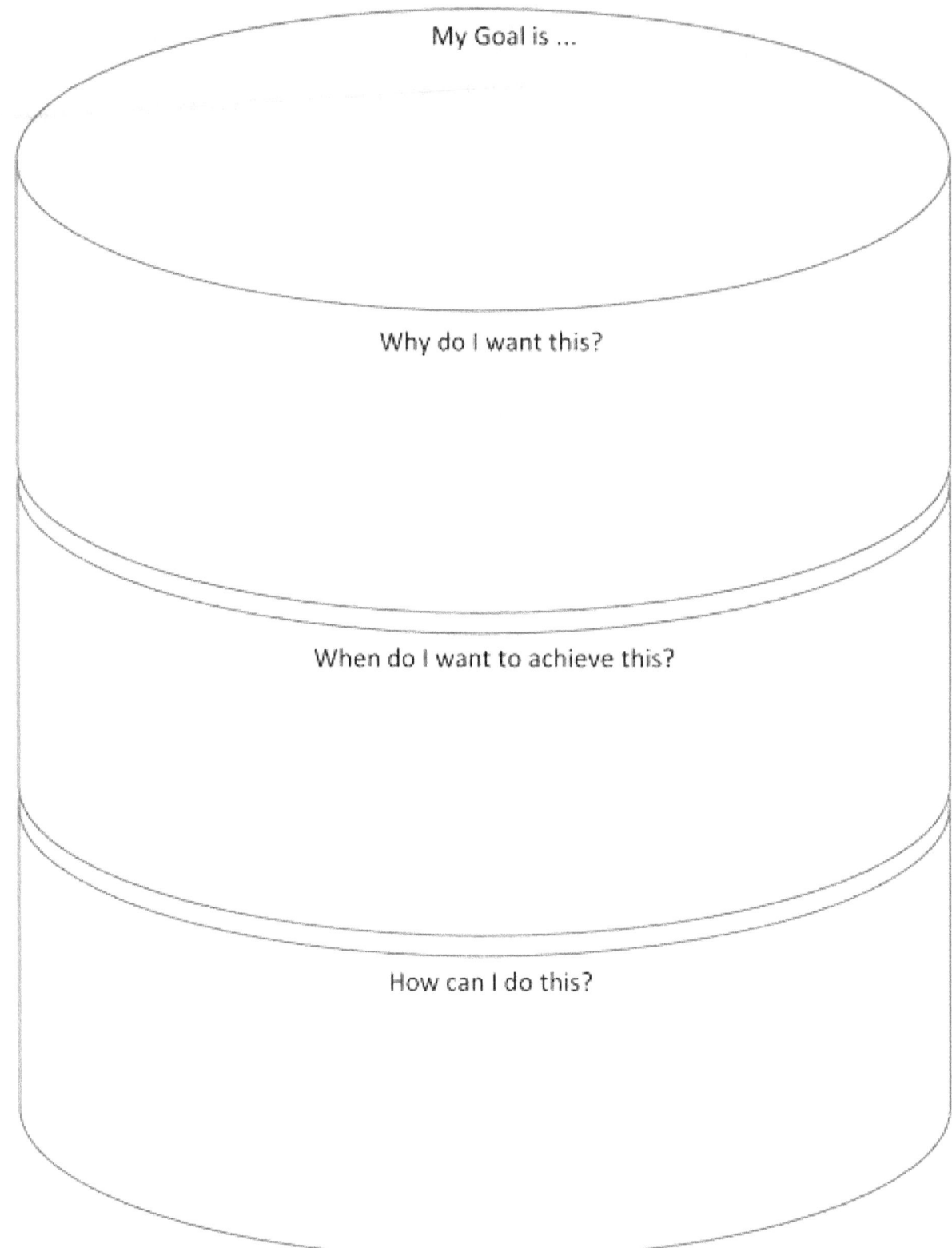

PRAY THE WORD

God's word is living and active. It is sharper than any two-edged sword and cuts as deep as the place where soul and spirit meet, the place where joints and marrow meet. God's word judges a person's thoughts and intentions." Hebrews 4:12 (GW)

Yes, I am a practical person but also a spiritual one, as any Christian should be. One year I decided that I would add more to my goals than just writing them out, working on them and praying about them. I decided to delve into the word of God to see if my goals aligned to the His word and visa verse. We have always heard that there is a Word for every situation in our lives and at the time I started this search, I really needed to know what God said concerning my life and the circumstances I faced. So for every goal, I selected 2 to 4 Bible verses and would make this a part of my prayer time. Certainly, I have seen the results of doing this, not only answered prayers but specific direction at times when I need it most.

For example, if I am praying about my child's wellbeing, one verse that I pray is Luke 2:52 that she would "increase in wisdom (in broad and full understanding) and in stature and years, and in favor with God and man." And indeed, I have seen my child develop in these areas throughout the years I have been praying this Word over her life.

I encourage you to spend some time studying the word of God and learn what promises the Lord has for you this year. Pray the Word and see the power of God at work transforming you and others. This kind of prayer moves you from concentrating on what is wrong in your life to seeing life from God's perspective.

My Prayer Strategy

Take a Personal Retreat

Life can get really hectic and exhausting to say the least. Sometimes you need a "time out". I have found that going on weekend retreats (usually a church event) to be renewing. Although those retreats often could be full of activity, I would try to find time alone at the end of the day to reflect and get God's direction for my future.

A personal retreat is a little different in that it's you and you alone with God. It does not have to be for a long period but it needs to be meaningful to you and you need to be able to come back to life renewed. Much can get in the way of doing "alone time" so it is best to plan ahead. If you are the type who needs the "company" maybe you can partner with a friend to do this. Just be sure to stay focused on the goal of the retreat - rest, spiritual renewal and revival, regeneration and direction.

My Personal Retreat

When?	
How long?	
Where?	
What will I do?	

Now go put this in your calendar. Plan now to make it happen!

GET ACCOUNTABLE

Two people are better than one because together they have a good reward for their hard work. If one falls, the other can help his friend get up. But how tragic it is for the one who is all alone when he falls. There is no one to help him get up. Again, if two people lie down together, they can keep warm, but how can one person keep warm? Though one person may be overpowered by another, two people can resist one opponent. A triple-braided rope is not easily broken. — Ecclesiastes 4:9-12 (GW)

Quite typical of human nature, we begin to work on our goals with excitement and start to see growth but as time goes on we may find ourselves waning a bit or not making any progress at all. This is understandable. We are not meant to go it alone. That's not what God intended for any of His children.

Personally, I have noticed that working in groups where there is accountability and encouragement forces me to get things done that I have committed to. If I am working alone, the challenge is greater to discipline myself to do what I know I should do.

This year make every effort to find a like-minded friend or group to help you in the pursuit of your goals. Join or start a mastermind group of people with similar interests to yours and who want to develop personally. The value of a strong friendship or accountability partner is priceless. You need that kind of support especially if you have struggled in the past to achieve your goals or if you strongly desire greater progress this year.

Write a list of friends or associates either in church, at work or otherwise that may be interested in connecting with you on a consistent basis (say, weekly) to discuss your goals progress and hold each other accountable for the goals you've committed to.

Alternatively, do some research and based on the goals you have outlined, find a local or online group with similar interests that you can participate in. If you are unable to do this, consider prayerfully starting a group. There are several resources online about how to start a mastermind group.

Consider taking action on one of these options:

1. Talk to one or two of your close friends about working together to help each other accomplish your goals. Encourage him/her to complete this workbook and set a date to discuss your goal list and your next steps. Try to meet weekly in person or by phone to keep track of each other's progress.

2. Contact five to seven potential friends or associates and discuss starting a group immediately. You can meet weekly; have everyone discuss their goals and progress and use books or other materials that would enhance your personal development. You can do this online or meet at a coffee shop or somewhere that is mutually convenient for all and that won't distract from your purpose.

"Where no wise guidance is, the people fall, but in the multitude of counselors there is safety." Prov. 11:14 (AMP)

My Support Team

1.
2.
3.
4.
5.
6.
7.
8.
9.
10.

WEEKLY, MONTHLY & QUARTERLY PLANNING

"Setting a goal is not the main thing. It is deciding how you will go about achieving it and staying with that plan." Tom Landry

In order to remain focused you need to set aside time at the beginning of each week to outline what you will do to get closer to your goals. When you do this, please factor in time for prayer, bible study, your family and time to rest. One simple practice to ensure that you don't burn out is to take one or two 15-min breaks during the day away from your work, your computer or anything that requires your full attention and energy. Just relaxing for a few minutes can boost your energy levels and creativity.

Consider planning on a big scale starting with 90-day goals and then break those down into monthly, weekly and daily steps. As you make your plans consider your day-to-day responsibilities and limit yourself to a manageable number of tasks. You know yourself and the commitments that you have on a daily basis; please don't over burden yourself.

On a quarterly basis you may aim to complete 2 or 3 major items on your dream list. Then during the 30-day challenges you can break them down into what you can handle considering all the other commitments and responsibilities you will have to do during that time. When you look at what you want your week to be like, you can outline smaller steps based on the 30-challenge. If you think you can handle 7 goal-oriented tasks a day or for a week, well then go ahead. If you can handle just one or two, then do so.

You may also consider doing your tasks based on time. For example, you may be able to commit 10 to 15 hours a week on a specific goal and therefore allocate your time on daily habits that make that happen. In all this planning, don't over-extend yourself and always ask God for wisdom.

So move into this year with a set of manageable steps towards your goals and trust God to help you through each stage. Listen closely as He guides you and make changes, where needed.

Note: Only a 90-day planner is included in this workbook. You may find it more practical to continue with a typical planner or an electronic one. The main goal of this workbook is to get you started on the right track. Beyond the 90 days, you will always use this as your point of reference for your plans going forward.

I am cheering you on all the way. Keep pressing ahead and receive the prizes and surprises that God has in store for you along this success journey.

JOURNAL YOUR THOUGHTS

"Documenting little details of your everyday life becomes a celebration of who you are." — *Carolyn V. Hamilton, Art Improv 101: How to Create a Personal Art Journal.*

I know you may be saying that this is a lot of work – a lot of thought, a lot of prayer and much writing have already gone into this workbook. But really, this is your life and if you want to experience **SUCCESSFUL LIVING**, you need to take time out to build it every day. So this is not just about completing this workbook but about building your life with every effort and energy you have to be the best YOU God designed you to be.

Having said that ☺ here is another step you can take towards succeeding in life – Journaling. It's an optional, you don't have to but oh how good it is the write your thoughts down. I don't do this every day or even every week but I do journal. I like to express my thoughts in writing. To me it is very therapeutic and relaxing for the soul. It relieves me of the many thoughts and emotions going on inside of me and frees me to express myself without the judgement of another. **Journaling has its benefits which I won't go into detail about here but just a few to note:**

- Journaling helps you to express your inner thoughts
- You are free to share who you are with you and with God and no one else
- It clears your mind of the clutter of the day or the week and positions you to a place of gratitude
- You learn that life isn't so bad and that you doing some things right

I would encourage you to consider this especially when you're feeling a bit weighted down with life's happenings. I have left some space at the end of each week for you to journal. Be free to add more pages if you wish.

Think about these questions if you're wondering what you can journal about:

- What did I accomplish since my last journal note that I am proud of?
- Did I do anything (no matter how small or big) to bring me closer to any of my goals?
- Where there any significant heart issues or personal encounters that I need to be address or pray about?
- What and who am I thankful for and why?
- What should I pray about going forward - goal, tasks, challenges, relationships, etc.?

With this questions to start you off on the journaling journey, go ahead - **Journal Your Success Journey**!

90-Day Review & Plan: _____

What Do I Want to Achieve this Quarter?

At the start of each quarter it's time to review and reorganize where needed. It's time to review what you've done so far as well as time to reflect, pray and give thanks to God for what He has done in your life. Remember whatever you have been able to do it is all by His grace and His strength.

It would be a good idea to start your review about 7 days before the quarter ends. By this time most of the quarter is completed and you have a good idea of what else you would be able to complete before the quarter ends. You would also start thinking of what the next quarter holds for you – what you would continue working on and if there are new adventures (goals) you would like to undertake. So mark your calendar for each quarterly review and planning time.

What goals did I reach last quarter?

_____
_____
_____
_____
_____
_____

What am I most thankful to God for (including unplanned successes and blessings)?

_____
_____
_____
_____
_____
_____

What did I do to celebrate the successes and blessings I received?

In the next 90-day season, what goals do I want to work on?

What steps can I take to help me accomplish these goals?

What resources (people, physical, financial) do I need to help me accomplish these goals?

30-Day Challenge – Month: _____

I call this a challenge because I want you to make every effort to get closer to your goals. Have fun along the way, learn from the highs and lows but don't get stressed out. Keep seeking God in all you do and He will give you success.

Ask yourself the following questions as you embark on this 30-day journey:

- What do I need to accomplish in the next 30 days to get closer to my goals?
- What are the top 4-7 tasks related to my goals that I need to work on in the next 30 days?
- What resources do I need (e.g. people, knowledge, materials)?
- Do I need to spend money to make things happen? Do I have enough money?
- Will I need to ask someone for help (free or swap services) or will I need to hire someone (expense)?

What do I need to do in the next 30 days to get closer to my goals?	Priority	Wk. 1	Wk. 2	Wk. 3	Wk. 4	Wk. 5	Resources needed

Month: _____

Sunday	Monday	Tuesday	Wednesday	Thursday	Friday	Saturday

WEEK _____

Priority	Weekday?	Activity – tasks specific to your goals	Comments	Done?

Notes:

JOURNALING MY SUCCESS JOURNEY

Week ____

Priority	Weekday?	Activity – tasks specific to your goals	Comments	Done?

Notes:

Journaling My Success Journey

Week _____

Priority	Weekday?	Activity – tasks specific to your goals	Comments	Done?

Notes:

Journaling My Success Journey

WEEK _____

Priority	Weekday?	Activity – tasks specific to your goals	Comments	Done?

Notes:

Journaling My Success Journey

My Creative Space

30-Day Challenge – Month: _____

I call this a challenge because I want you to make every effort to get closer to your goals. Have fun along the way, learn from the highs and lows but don't get stressed out. Keep seeking God in all you do and He will give you success.

Ask yourself the following questions as you embark on this 30-day journey:

- What do I need to accomplish in the next 30 days to get closer to my goals?
- What are the top 4-7 tasks related to my goals that I need to work on in the next 30 days??
- What resources do I need (e.g. people, knowledge, materials)?
- Do I need to spend money to make things happen? Do I have enough money?
- Will I need to ask someone for help (free or swap services) or will I need to hire someone (expense)?

What do I need do in the next 30 days to get closer to my goals?	Priority	Wk. 1	Wk. 2	Wk. 3	Wk. 4	Wk. 5	Resources needed

MONTH: _____

Sunday	Monday	Tuesday	Wednesday	Thursday	Friday	Saturday

WEEK _____

Priority	Weekday?	Activity – tasks specific to your goals	Comments	Done?

Notes:

Journaling My Success Journey

WEEK _____

Priority	Weekday?	Activity – tasks specific to your goals	Comments	Done?

Notes:

JOURNALING MY SUCCESS JOURNEY

Week _____

Priority	Weekday?	Activity – tasks specific to your goals	Comments	Done?

Notes:

Journaling My Success Journey

Week _____

Priority	Weekday?	Activity – tasks specific to your goals	Comments	Done?

Notes:

JOURNALING MY SUCCESS JOURNEY

My Creative Space

30-Day Challenge – Month: _____

I call this a challenge because I want you to make every effort to get closer to your goals. Have fun along the way, learn from the highs and lows but don't get stressed out. Keep seeking God in all you do and He will give you success.

Ask yourself the following questions as you embark on this 30-day journey:

- What do I need to accomplish in the next 30 days to get closer to my goals?
- What are the top 4-7 tasks related to my goals that I need to work on in the next 30 days??
- What resources do I need (e.g. people, knowledge, materials)?
- Do I need to spend money to make things happen? Do I have enough money?
- Will I need to ask someone for help (free or swap services) or will I need to hire someone (expense)?

What do I need to do in the next 30 days to get closer to my goals?	Priority	Wk. 1	Wk. 2	Wk. 3	Wk. 4	Wk. 5	Resources needed

Month: _____

Sunday	Monday	Tuesday	Wednesday	Thursday	Friday	Saturday

WEEK _____

Priority	Weekday?	Activity – tasks specific to your goals	Comments	Done?

Notes:

Journaling My Success Journey

Week ____

Priority	Weekday?	Activity – tasks specific to your goals	Comments	Done?

Notes:

_____

_____

_____

_____

_____

JOURNALING MY SUCCESS JOURNEY

Make Your Year a Living Success Goals Workbook

WEEK _____

Priority	Weekday?	Activity – tasks specific to your goals	Comments	Done?

Notes:

_____

_____

_____

_____

_____

JOURNALING MY SUCCESS JOURNEY

Week _____

Priority	Weekday?	Activity – tasks specific to your goals	Comments	Done?

Notes:

Journaling My Success Journey

My Creative Space

This Year & Beyond – Your Life Story

"You are never too old to set another goal or to dream a new dream." <u>C. S. Lewis</u>

Here I want you to dream, not a little but a lot. Write your life story. Write a story of what your life looks like in the future. The catch – write it in present tense as if you are already living this life story.

Don't be hesitant about what you are writing. Feel free to dream and use extra pages to complete it if you need to. Also remember there may be some longer term goals (which are not one-year goals) that you haven't included in your plans for this year – try to include them in your life story.

As you do this be consciously aware that God knows the plans He has for you and that with the Holy Spirit in you, you can begin to see a glimpse of what your future looks like on paper.

Start writing…. On the next page.

Now that you have done that read it out loud at least 3 times and then as part of your daily or weekly routine read it again and again. This is your life. Sure some things will change or there may be diversions along the way or some major re-routing to do as the Lord leads but this is the beginning of living success with Christ. Use this as a catalyst to move you forward day after day.

> *"… You must love the Lord your God with all your heart and with all your soul and with all your strength and with all your mind; and your neighbor as yourself. And Jesus said to him, 'You have answered correctly; do this, and you will live [enjoy active, blessed, endless life in the kingdom of God]'." Luke 10:25-28 (AMP).*

My Life Story

Congratulations!

Congratulations and well done! You have stayed the course and have completed the initial work to your Living Success Year!

Please keep moving forward and in all you do love God, love others and yes love yourself and you will experience joy in life. Don't forget to rely on God's word as your source of strength, encouragement and direction. Also consider having a friend along with you (or join a group) on this goal-success journey for moral support and accountability.

Let this workbook and planner by your companion throughout the year. Don't forget you can pick up additional 90-day planning pages at this link (https://www.pamelavcarmichael.com/resources/living-success-goals-workbook-90-day-planning-sheets/). Keep this workbook close to hand to jot down your ideas and thoughts as well – make sure have a few extra blank pages strategically placed for this purpose.

I am really excited about this season. I see each day, week, month, quarter, special holiday and New Year as seasons of refreshing and as opportunities for good change. I especially love the "newness" feeling that the ushering in of a New Year brings. There is hope, new hope. There is an energy, renewed and new that spurs us to move forward. Use the hope and energy of this new season to start your year and ask the Lord to let His joy keep you going throughout this year and beyond.

May this be your best Living Success Year and the start of your best life ever in Christ!

Pamela Carmichael

Pamela Carmichael

"This Book of the Law shall not depart out of your mouth, but you shall meditate on it day and night, that you may observe and do according to all that is written in it. For then you shall make your way prosperous, and then you shall deal wisely and have good success." Josh. 1:8(AMP)

Please Share Your Experience

Write a Review

One more thing, before you go can I ask you for a quick favor?

Seeing that you have reached the end of this book, I can only conclude that you liked what you read and it was beneficial to you. At least I hope so ☺.

Please leave a review for this book on Amazon? I'd really appreciate it. Your review would not only help others decide if this book is right for them but it would help sell more books. This will in turn assist me to write more books for you.

To leave a review, go to https://www.amazon.com/dp/0991785037, scroll down the page and click on the "Write a customer review" button. From there you can select the star rating and write a short note about your experience with this book. If you used a different platform by all means you can leave a review there too!

Thank you for reading, and thank you so much for being part of this journey with me.

Share on Social Media

I'd also like to hear from you. It's encouraging to authors when readers comment about their work.

So send me a Tweet or Facebook posts. I am looking forward to hearing from you!

You can also connect with me via any other these social media platforms.

   https://www.facebook.com/PamelaVCarmichaelAuthor

   https://plus.google.com/+PamelaCarmichael

   https://twitter.com/PamvCarmichael

   http://www.pamelavcarmichael.com

Notes

OTHER RESOURCES

In this award winning title, *Financial Empowerment: Realign Your Finances to God's Will*, Pamela explores nine key areas of personal finance - creating wealth, tithing, saving, giving, investing, spending, borrowing, lending and planning. She examines the issues and misconceptions most experience in their finances and provides help with Biblical and practical solutions.

Financial Empowerment is the road map to personal and spiritual growth, financial well-being and a lifetime of empowerment through Godly principles.

Get your copy at https://www.amazon.com/

Pamela Carmichael is a passionate educator of financial empowerment for people. She produces workshops and seminars centred on financial literacy education.

Learn more at http://www.pamelavcarmichael.com/speaking/

Resume Writing | Cover Letter Writing | Follow-up & Thank You Letters | Career Success Plan | Career Coaching Services

Are you ready for a career change? Do you need help to land your next job? Do you want to get promoted?
Are you ready to earn want you're worth? Would you like to enjoy your work and not dread it?
But wait, is your resume ready? Or can you do with some help to get you started on your new career adventure?

Learn more at http://www.pamelavcarmichael.com/

ABOUT PAMELA
Speaker, Author, Coach

Pamela Carmichael is a passionate educator of financial empowerment for people. Her Financial Empowerment Initiative produces workshops and seminars centred on financial literacy education.

Pamela is concerned over the general lack of fundamental and basic financial education of both youth and adults. Pamela combines her passion to see others succeed with her 18+ years' experience in the financial services industry to train others to effectively manage their finances. Her concern for those who struggle financially led her to authoring the award-winning book titled *Financial Empowerment: Re-align Your Finances to God's Will*.

Pamela's desire to deliver quality financial education inspired her to gain the **Certified Financial Education Instructor** (National Financial Education Council) designation. She is also a member of the Personal Finance Speakers Association. Pamela conducts financial empowerment workshops, speaking events, money life coaching programs to help people move from financial struggle to success and significance. She also shares insights on her Living Success blog relating to managing your personal finances and to living successfully through the study and application of God's word.

Pamela has a Bachelor's degree in **Economics & Accounting** (University of the West Indies Cave Hill Campus) and has a successful career as a financial service professional with over 18 years' experience. Along with her financial education certification, she is also a **Certified Professional Coach** (Wainwright Global, Inc.; Institute of Professional Coaching) and a **Success Principles Certified Coach**.

An author, a teacher, an encourager, a coach and more, Pamela combines her passion for financial empowerment along with her experience and training in financial services, financial education and life coaching to educate and motivate people to take action toward achieving financial freedom and personal success that multiplies into positive changes in society.

Connect with Pamela:

 https://www.facebook.com/PamelaVCarmichaelAuthor

 https://plus.google.com/+PamelaCarmichael

 https://twitter.com/PamvCarmichael

 http://www.pamelavcarmichael.com

www.ingramcontent.com/pod-product-compliance
Lightning Source LLC
Chambersburg PA
CBHW080348170426
43194CB00014B/2729